Kalagora

Siddhartha Bose is a poet and performer based in London. He grew up in India, followed by a seven year stint in the USA. Selections of his work have appeared in the anthologies *City State: New London Poetry* (Penned in the Margins, 2009), *Voice Recognition: 21 Poets for the 21st Century* (Bloodaxe Books, 2009) and *The HarperCollins Book of Modern Poetry in English by Indians* (HarperCollins, 2010).

Bose has recently completed a PhD at Queen Mary, University of London. His one-man stage show, *Kalagora*, was produced by Penned in the Margins and received its premiere in London in 2010. He is developing a full-length play with WhynotTheatre, Toronto, and was dubbed one of the 'ten rising stars of British poetry' by *The Times*.

kalagora.com

Kalagora
Siddhartha Bose

Penned in the Margins
LONDON

PUBLISHED BY PENNED IN THE MARGINS
53 Arcadia Court, 45 Old Castle Street, London E1 7NY
www.pennedinthemargins.co.uk

All rights reserved

© Siddhartha Bose

The right of Siddhartha Bose to be identified as the author of this work has been asserted by him in accordance with Section 77 of the Copyright, Designs and Patent Act 1988.

This book is in copyright. Subject to statutory exception and to provisions of relevant collective licensing agreements, no reproduction of any part may take place without the written permission of Penned in the Margins.

First published 2010

ISBN
978-0-9565467-4-6

This book is sold subject to the condition that it shall not, by way of trade or otherwise, be lent, re-sold, hired out, or otherwise circulated without the publisher's prior consent in any form of binding or cover other than that in which it is published and without a similar condition including this condition being imposed on the subsequent purchaser.

Acknowledgements

The author is grateful to the editors of the following journals and anthologies, where poems from this book have appeared: *Alhamra Literary Review, City State: New London Poetry, Eclectica, Fulcrum, The HarperCollins Book of Modern English Poetry by Indians, The Literary Review, Litro, Likestarlings, Soundings, Tears in the Fence, Times Online, Voice Recognition: 21 Poets for the 21st Century, The Yellow Nib, The Wolf.*

Thanks to James Byrne and all the poets in *The Wolf* workshops in '07 and '08. Thanks to Tom Chivers for keeping me visible, as well as Stephen Watts, Anthony Joseph, Ahren Warner, Rustom Bharucha and Christopher Merrill.

Stories in the book are intertwined with the lives of others. Thanks to Jacqueline Bose in particular for her support and friendship. Thanks also to Phyllis Bose (and Ruby Bose, in memory). Special thanks to Shatadru Sarkar and Atish Ghosh. My endless gratitude to my mother, Sushmita Bose, for always being there. And Maria Tzika, for love and friendship.

This book is for my father, who opened the doors.

AUTHOR'S NOTE

Kalagora has grown with me for many years. It has been conceived and written across three continents.

The 'Animal City' of the book is Bombay, city of my childhood. Many other cities have contributed to its inception including New York, Columbus, Bangalore and, above all, Calcutta, city of my birth, and London, where this book became what it is.

Kalagora is a Hindi neologism that translates as 'black man/white man'.

This book tells his story.

Contents

I..... Prolectric

    Kalagora   15

II.... Sunya

    Little Taste   21
    Journey   22
    Schooldays   23
    Romanticism   25
    Nameless   29
    Sleepless (in America)   33
    Wandering shadow   34
    Proposal   36
    Sex and the City   37
    Back and Forth   38
    Swansong, Mile End   39
    East Village, New York   40
    Entracte   41

III.... Maya

    Sketching   47
    Eye Candy   53
    Hampi (Ruins)   58
    Garden, Bangalore   60
    Still Life: Artichoke   61

Triangle	62
Shoreditch Serenade	64

IV.... Nagri

Prologue/novel	73
Animal City	75
Finding Time	81
Chinatown, New York	82
Benares	83
Portrait, Little Lane, Calcutta	86
Istanbul, November, '03	87
Mother's Lament	89

V.... Epilepsis

Sketching (slight return)	93

Kalagora

Do you know what we are? They are wise and they tell us there is a new species on this earth. It is not this or that, it belongs not here or there, it is nothing. In the beginning when we were born, Sanjay, we were just what we were, the sons of our mothers and fathers, but now we are something else. But time has passed and the years have made us a new animal: chi-chi, half-and-half, black-and-white. Do you know what this means, black-and-white?

— Vikram Chandra, *Red Earth and Pouring Rain*

For

Shyamal Kumar Bose

(1950 – 2008)

father, philosopher, guide

I

Prolectric

Kalagora

I

Been given a set o' mirrors, a
net o' raw reflecting jewels,
cut crystal ruins o' billboards,
dustbins, cars, caravans o' meat,
computer chips, shards to
clay, soap operas,
wheels o' fire, statue rituals —

been smoked o' herb, witch, junk, pills, the
lot. Been made the god o' monkey, been told to
squeeze out oil o' ma veins, pore o' ma lobes, to
strike match altars and build
towers o' words in
clothes o' clown stripped o' language, home,
made many o' accent with ten heads,
to reflect, with gaunt o' breath o' rain,
alien worlds — story boxes — in glass that
slashes my wrists.

> I heard the leper o' Calcutta say,
> the bowl o' her hands cradling the city,
> the soul o' monsoon wind, her voice —
>
> 'The holy stains

the need, the hour.'

And O' so me a c-c-caterpillar, not
yet a b-b-butterfly, cocooned in
confines o' brick,
sitting 'midst straws o' iron,
shells o' sulphur,
quicksilver graffiti,
open wounds, aaaaaaart.

In immaculate gestation
I bounced round the oceans
o' the Earth, and like my wandering shadow,
sowed cemeteries in
        animal cities.

Yet, I come clear —

        my tales lung others.

So I hide behind a curtain,
fall asleep, snore.

    II

In my tapestry o' dreams
I'm at a theatre,
covered in hill, tree, a river o' diamonds, a

sky bleached brass.

I'm not alone —
to my right, a brown king
draped in spots o' red is
eaten by black horses —

    blood sprays. They rip
    flesh, chew with hints.

To my left, a gathering o' sun ra trumpets
played by robed black women
greets this serenade, this gluttony.

A thunderclap o' applause
spreads like plaguefire as many
in blue jeans,
masks o' rotting wood chiselled to smiles
begin to laugh, pricked
    by farce.

I noticed myself nude,
hid in
bushes o' hair,
my cock jutting out
like a promontory.

Laughter smells as a
man with black beard,

Caliban's curse, enters from
        backstage left.

With a wand o' hair
he plucks another
mask from the air round us,
and with smile o' passion
on red wrinkled face, he
holds it to me, this magic
mask o' mud,
        o' my shame—

eyes large, luminous, like

        the moon on a night
        o' scorching, pagan rites.

II

Sunya

Little Taste

    Mamallapuram —

in rock,
God sleeps on a ten-head snake, black in iron.

Sighs, wakes, lifts in curls of smoke,
rattles —

    (apsaras drench the sky with stones,
        sadhus fling flowers –rosepetal, saffronstain, lilyweb —
    from a cloud).

    Manhattan —

a woman spread on 4th street.

Grain of sand in white hair,
eyes blank, tear-swell,
as she hikes her skirt, nonchalant, to
piss on the sidewalk —

    eaten by sirens,
    marched upon by clean, shined feet.

Journey

the boy hears
voices holy as the
chime of bells

the boy sees
on a coal train
rushing through the
lungs of his country

a gathering of
nine still cranes
swanwhite

formed in a circle round a
pool of clear, stagnant water

Schooldays

And there were three of them,
back at old Anglican school in Bombay —
the bald man who picked his nostrils
(rolling balls of snot in forefinger and thumb);
the fat woman in short, polka-dotted skirt (eyes flayed, smile in
                                            fist), who
wailed like Nargis;
and the other old witch, buckteeth and hairy hands.
I told them I wanted to study the
Philosophy of History. They
kicked me in the stomach for it
(an answer of some elegance, yes…?).
Baldie, with face a cockroach,
bulged eyeballs, broke his rusty ruler on my neck.
They forced me down on all fours —
fatty seated herself on my back
blowing a marching bugle,
while the witch brought a knife to my throat
(I pissed my pants, no disrespect ma!).
Baldie dried his wagging tongue on his fingers —
he pulled down my blue wet trousers,
licking his lips, pushing his dusty crusty forefinger up my arse.
After much inspection,
he dragged out my intestines,
which were long and bent — the
colour of rainbows.

A cloud of flies burst on these organs
while the three archangels chanted in unison,
"Boys will be boys."

Romanticism

I

I woke, *silent as a stone*, to
glimpse a palpitating star,
drop diamonds
on the streetcrack of New Alipore.

(Maa, baba slept in mosquito nets,
coiled in dreams.)

Flowers of iron, sacks of shit,
burnt bridges of neglect
stared back at me with grins
as I struggled to light the bits
of a dogeared joint.

A barebodied driver
slept on his diseased yellow taxi,
arms flailing to windwipe the
odour of mosquitoes.
Somewhere a raga rose and fell, its
strains leaping out of a grilled, netted window.

The whirring of a creaking fan
gonged my ears.

I scratched my balls,
throbbing with heat.

I watched a moth of a man
emerge from the hide of a shop shutter,
a worn out blanket of clothes on his body. He crossed the street to
stare, tug, yell at a communist banner.

Under a halo, herdsmen
beat lambs marked in pink circles.

II

I crouch in a dazzling couch of grass,
spotted like a leopard, with flowers.
On me and around
falls a drizzle of rain,
drops coloured in bold, heavy as oil,
strapped to the orange of a sagging sky.

Before me there shints a tapestry of trees
engraved to a cradle of rocks.

In the distance tigers groan, beautiful.

Bright, flapping birds roam on a dripping sun.

The cackling of crystals

folds this pastoral scene—

a raw rattle of jewels.

I notice a small Hindu temple
sculpted in stone
telling of lovers and animals—

they run about in squirrels chasing scraps of food,
lips blowing fumes of contorted body parts.

In a frieze curtained in tombs, a
dog licks the honey of a courtesan. She
becomes a goddess, winking.

Their heads are tropical nights.

A small fire chokes the rain.
A woman dark as urnash,
my own *belle dame* of oceans and stories,
melts to existence
from the universe of a temple wall—

robed in pearls, hair weaving
tales in the wind,
she walks me, eyes wide as my mouth,
lips streaked in pleasure;

her face soaks in the

sweat of fever.

      'Will you burn my bones?
      Chop my nails?
      Sliver my eyes?
      Float me Ganga?'

The rain
      strikes petals.

Mind bursts like a star —

I fall on a bed of crows —

black milk of my scars.

    III

A baby roared in sleep,
while dogs outside my window talked in hieroglyphs.

Fought for pieces of shattered, rotten bread.

Nameless

I

I was always an accomplice actor.

In my onewindowed room
I heard voices at weddings in
cities where mothers know the
glint of the moon, the spark of the cold.

These chants soar high to the
cracks in my ceiling; become the ravens of
Beethoven's last quartets; choruses to a goddess
by the Ganges, her skin as silt, black—her
tongue limp, red with shame.

A fine wedding this—
fugues of blood.

II

Shhh...

red wine, a mosquito bite on my hand.

The rattle of rifles—sporadic

rain that summer — outside our
home in Calcutta —
a communist city,
no place for faith.

In the north a mosque was raped.

The city shuts. My mother eats the curls of her hair.
Hear the guns, shona! Hear the guns!
A child of twelve.

In my father's absence, I invoke
a street named after Ghalib where I was
greeted with a smile by a leper
balding with disease, her arms
hanging like carcasses, her teeth
black, her eyes — sweating streets
of the city — crowded, with flies.

She held a dog's mouth in her fist.
Not alive, not dead.

The city forms in veins.
Cut open.

III

I saw her for the next five months.

She watched me, sniffing—a
huntsman on all fours—rain,
sweat, typhoid, falling from my
skin in bombs.

IV

*Hungry. Need medicine. Crack
my knuckles. Gets
cold at night. Mosquitoes. Pirates. Planes.
Flies on muttonsticks.
Partition. Brothers shaved my head. Others tied
me by the legs. Whipped me. My nostrils groaned.
The smell of coalmines.*

Poisha dao!

*The whiff of sandstone –
in Rajasthan, had mirrors on my dress.
A woman, pale skin, straddled the seas, gave it me.
Draped on head by wave of silk,
red and yellow long snake on my lap...*

V

I wade past whores,
darkred bangles clattering,

men with needles in their arms seated round a temple like lotuses;
a rickshawpuller who starts selling hash, changes his name,
becomes a Hindu just before the fast;

couples stepping out of Japanese cars,
to make it on time for
rehearsals of Chekhov's short stories and plays.

VI

Shhh...

I write to her, my Kali Maa.
Smug. (A can of soup, in America.)

Not alive, not dead.

Sleepless (in America)

—Paganini was a promulgator of fiddle fodder, says the man who crosses Dolphy and a swallow. No jazz fo him tho. He a violin virtuoso, fifty an nine years. He been called a nigga in his time. He crosses swords in his eye. He bury in Dickens and the stock market. He singing, he dancing, he fretting with butterfly hands, and honeys me with a Bachnote drone.

—No! I'd not give my years to Paganini! *But*...to sit in a room with Beethoven, to hear him play the late quartets, to squeeze out the cosmos o' his mind from his blind, dead ears... *that* would be somethin I tell ya!

I look round the bar, and look into me. I've drunk a litre of special scotch, coz I got paid today. I been at the corner of high st, shootin some bad pool. I'm drinking long island ice-teas, like I used to with Lulu, who'd walk a dog she called 'Tiger'. In a few hours, I'll clean the place with Christoph who'll tell me tales of Albania, o' changing his name in Greece coz they don't like the prophet there, o' how his dad died a week after he left, o' how he ain't seen his mum in fifteen years, o' how his girl bluesed him over, o' how he cokes himself to sleep, and I know the musician with hairs of regret comin out his eyes will smell like an old lost friend in Brooklyn who'd roll down sidewalk night after night, the cuts on his face soaked in whiskey.

I tell ya, I dialect my soul thru foreign sounds. There's no, I'm sho, India in this skin.

Wandering shadow

You, a vagabond midst rock 'n'rollers.

Suedemind you wink into slit of morning—grayskulled weather. Your booze 'o breath bombinates your room—

greased plates coughed like phlegm from sink. Red bloods on eggs. Flying saucer o' glass glints in iced vodka. Torn books grunt. Ash burns in carpet, hash embers. Coltrane shifts like workers, squeals like pigs. Your body fjords. Candlewax foams your eyes.

A fly climbs up blinds, wakes windowpanes, falls. Repeat. Infinite rain.

You stungun in walk. You pour a drink—crash 'n' burn, scratch a sore, blister. A cloud throats in your mouth, drizzle dreams.

The money you own is a drink. You donate blood plasma. Skin ripples in gas. Your friends are housepainters, acidshone armythumping hippies, a Russian refugee from Azerbaijan who wears a mohawk, raped by an uncle when he was ten.

In Chicago, mates play jazz, or get stuck on dope.

You shit, and blood spurts. You aren't very well.

A friend burns your house. You've strange luck with girls.

You've shorn opium dens, slick o' dragon air souled your eyes. Your nails grow plants. Your feet are jelly.

When you dream you meet a statuegod from the sea (who says life is suffering), get shot in the back o' your head by blackmasked men on tanks like driftwood on a Bombay stream

(riot of noise. Chinese dive with mirrors for windows. you see yourself pinged by the hard electricity of a bullet. air leaks from your balloon skin. you float off your mattress, awake, feeling the split in the back of your skull. you cry for home.)

Somedays you forget to eat. You spend all your time in bars. You know you're killing yourself but you can't stop. Otherdays you're running from the cops, working shifts selling cleanass ammonia drugs to midwesterners who've skinned god alive like a mango peeled, mainlined him into the cross of their dna, triphipping him up like fashion. You need their cash, you spit in your mind.

Nights you wander. A witch from Tennessee cocks you up at a greyhound bustop, takes you home. Your friends come over and play African drums. She sings, takes you makes you fresh. Morning, your skin sliced like a lemon, you leave, a slip o' Dylan on your tongue.

These stories will last. You need more time to tell them proper, you say, entering the clean shave of a motel room, sirens ringing in the distance, the cum of war, splattered.

Proposal

In the old days at the
        wet bus-stop,
                you said to me

                (a smile on
                your face
                like a siren):

'Together we swallow the sun and the moon.

Blame God for
        cramps, diarrhoea, exile. We

                              shit horses. Puke
                                  electricity.'

Sex and the City

She brings me striped shirts cos her father wore them, my love in the afternoon. Blue and white stripe Calcutta—enter her parlour shocked with revolving wooden chandelier darting spots of light, dust in light.
She maps me in her web, spinning limbs.
—Give give, I'll do, she groans in that salt tone, as she grips me in skin that bubbles in sores. Some like galaxies sweat pus, not stars. Room is wet with rain that never comes. The floor heaves under us, instinctive as nitrate.
A Tom Waits razor growl chops me up.
I lie on her single bed the clay of hash in my hair. Black and wet like Kali, she plays the piston.
I am stung on a rack, flayed.
We go to a play by a temple, and as the blackyellow cab turns to Ballygunge by the kebab shop with men wrapped in loincloth, passing the day watching smoke gather on tram tracks, we see two stray dogs doing what is natural with an insistence that frightens, as we hike up our reserve in a giddy laughter.
Not in London— dogs fucking, fleas on backs, stone as my pocket of alley in the east end, which is home more or less than home. Sometimes, on a late Saturday when the gods crawl outta their holes, I see a man taking the piss by a bin, and the smell, not the trickle—a branch of veins—reminds me of where I'm from, and I glow like a lantern, holy.

Back and Forth

A man, a boy (one bearded, the other with rings in hair) meet once a week for Moroccan tea jasmine smile, prance updown conversation scales (odd jobs, fraught infidelities, leaving London), tire to statues after hours, turn up Manu Chau, catpoise, shut the old white wooden bedroom door, cradle, and trail a football, not daring to lift their eyes that crawl along feet (no, not eye alone, but vein, hip, the tip of freefall hair, dripglue spit), constant like metronomes, handing the ball back with such care that I, a subtenant subhuman migrant scum with holes in grey corduroys in room with red 'n' blue curtains much too large for window, breathe alone, so alone—a green plant, chewing carbon.

Swansong, Mile End

Pigeons on a tiled roof.
Foreground—bus stop shines in the rain.

Swans—patches of cloud—
float along Regent's Canal, its

skin, moving fish scales.

Shirt of sky opens.
Hair of stars sprout.

Plastic bags crackle like
pellets of rain in a tin can, like fire

bled in wood.

A southbound train lunges over a
bridge.

The night is radioactive.

The two swans screech their song of love,
shake their manes,

proud as horses.

East Village, New York

The moment's mischief—

leafshadows of sun
crack open sixpack clouds,
fill spaces in
tense brittle treefingers,
bulb on a naked priest at the
corner of St. Mark's,
grant him
robe of sun, halo of dust
for a little performance, seethed and
bruised:

a tiredrunk Bird—

      'I remember, o' lawd, in ma father's house,
         Ma father's house'—

a new revolution
    soak his chant—

        'Da new world, it gonna come'—

his back a salute,
    eyes closed, hat in hand.

Entracte

Nighthawks in Larry's Bar, Columbus

—It's so hard to listen to
Bach these days. My fridge hums,
the TV's too fuckin loud,
my neighbor sneezes
with holy passion.
—I cut out lines from the
newspaper—random, you knooooooaw...
then made a rhyme scheme outta that,
eh voila!
—How d'ya do it?
—Talent's rare, mon cher...
—Preludes and fugues...
so warm, so nice...
—Who said that, Apollinaire?
—And moral responsibility?
—The pisser's over there...
—And the role of ethics?
—Bladder's full, yes...
—And the question of karma?
—I want to sleep...
—One can't objectify sensation...
—In harpsichord or piano?
—With three girls last night maan, but ma
dad wants me to go to laaaw school...

—I'm all about Locke, you know...
—I don't know...
—Piano, piano of course!
—But I might go to laaaw school...
—Sir John to the pool
   table please!
—I'm a mother of a nine month
   old baby, and my husband's
   Greek, so I stay at home often...
—I love women
   with heavy hands...
—Tonight he let me loose...
—And a big mothafuckin ass...
—And I'm as free as a cat...
—I didn't like Noo Yawk as much as that,
   I prefer smaller places, now
   I got a grandchild...
—Pork and beans make me fart...
—Poetry has to start
   from a philosophical basis, it
   can't do without philosophy, but it
   don't work the
   other way round...
—I hate sushi...
—I'm in fashion bitch...
—'Scool 'scool 'scool
—And personal poetry is in vogue
   as of late...
—To eat with chopsticks man...

—Melancholic postmodern piddle...
—I really *do* play bass well...
—The length of the pole...
—A Japanese poet once said...
—Is proportionate to the breadth of the hole!
  Heee heee ahhhha hhaaaa!
—And I fuckin dig Dolphy maaan...
—That the souls of man and wife in love
  bend towards each other like bending
  weeds in the sea...
—Newtonian of course...
—And he said other wonderful things
  about falling cherry blossoms and the
  smells of chrysanthemums and plum trees...
—By choice, not by force...
—He didn't need newspapers you see
—Fiddle dee dee...

(A man with flowers in hand, enters,
Led by a dog)

—I, blind as Dhritarashtra, have
  come to tell you all
  the world is dark, very dark—
  and I am all outta quarters!

III

Maya

(Animal)

Sketching

I

The sidewalk's a midget.

New Year's Eve, New York.

'Don't trust noone else,' she says,
shooting him with her skin, sinking neck,
bones like altars.

'All this fo real, fo sho.'

II

He wants to be a god, Shivasexy.
His arm
sliced, his stomach lining dragged by a bear's hand, his
throat a canary outside a
bar in the freeze of 9th and Avenue A, he
lights a match on the stone steps of his welcoming, and
waves it to a gypsy by a dustbin,
like a wand.

'Even the drug's more white here than brown...
pure, phenyl swept, unhybrid.'

III

She holds, like a bell jar, the crustcrumbs of his country,
brownred earth heaving before monsoon rain:

clouds crowblack, runny like eggs, so close to the hairy coconuts of
                                          palm trees that
she touches them, tears out a spidershape from the sky which sticks to her
palms like candyfloss.

The earth is heavenly —

smells of wet hair,
fossil fumes, piss.

IV

She holds brown crumbles on a
foilsheet, tinlike, concentric circles made by fire
blue as a heron's underwing.

She folds into he, vaporfree:

boiling black fluid takes flight,
slips to a dragon's snare, a lion's roar.

taste softens, puke gathers.

In a dream sudden as winter light on the
bits of a leaf's hair, a
bird, pigeon perhaps, applauds.

He wipes ash from his eye.

V

She takes him to a room with a chair, a boxer dog, a red curtain.
A stretcher for
canvasses and dead bodies.
A gaslit lantern hums. The floor
crawls with black ants. Each time they step
their legs feel like astronauts.

VI

Stubble drifts through her voice:

'Seal your events to a stone.
then you'll evolve.
Waiting to exhale, you now know you
tasted the peel of your liver, bloated like a Chinese mushroom.
You now feel the sweat in your spine
coagulate in sharp crystals.
You'd never have no balls to stick nails in yer arm,

crucifried.'

VII

He smells unda curry, which shades to fresh grass,
stunned still by the lisp of coming rain.

She beats him with her scars.
coats wounds with gin.
bandages with barbed wire.

They blow — to each other — their souls in
mirrors of rain.

VIII

They walk together, upstream,
tigers stitched to their red dreams.
She teaches, he learns.
She grows into the silence of wood, painting
scenes like saris, necks in arches, a
mermaid from saltwaters. Her brush is gold.

He, hit by book, makes noise, fills a cup with wind,
chops words in words:

'So poets write of Basho

talking to wooden huts, cherry blossom, falling chrysanthemum.
I tried, I failed.

I make use of what's available today:

cramped rooms, immigration officers

—You mooozlim?
—No.
—Hindu?
—Could say.
—Practising?
—Whatchya mean?
—You speak English very well.
—Whose?
—What?
—Don't ghabraofy boss, sahi hai. Me got style. Capisci?

A man in grey jumper at the edge of a
park, head in hands, a half-empty Hallers glinting in a sun
thick with butter.'

IX

'Remember,' she spawns simply—

'experience is the form of sympathy.'

They occupy a country caught in the

shifts of tectonic plates.

On a cold knifenight in
New York, the city's city —

the midget's grown.

Eye Candy

I

Your eyes glove
thorns (open close, open
close, swinging door) —

I pluck one
out, swallow.

I work in negatives,
                map outlines.

II

You came to me infold o' flower,
mole on your left breast.

I promised you on a
        rainlit
                pebble of a day, the
        sun would thaw in my tongue.

You came to,
        I promise, in starch
            of a dream, your hair, creviced curls, a parched

      blank papyrus in the
      crawl of your hands,

your hair
      spread in legs, reaching
           out to me like strong spider.

This dream—

hole in mist, light in chloroform,
leaf in synthesis, soaked in sepia,
      plod afterglow.

You came in blank
      papyrus, showing me words,
           gift of rain, glowing me—

the greatest poem of all.

           Cloud
                mother o' mountain
           rain
                glut o' treespring

                monsoon man,
           peacock on brow, you
           hunt feathers in the dawn.

           Lift me mount me,

> *a consort courtesan, so I*
> *form myself in Shivacurls,*
> *bending to rock, arching to bow, I*
> *flow through gates and forests,*
> *crash to dungbeetle, firefly, moth,*
> *piedog, python,*
> *tiger, lulled to the sex of the bay...*

III

In a village by Napoli, they say

> *When you see her you'll know...*

    I saw you, I know.

Partition my body, like my country:
    heart to my wife, gizzard to my mum, liver to my son.

    Oh god, why am I me?

IV

On a foggyday (in Londontown —
in Mile End, the bridge a rainbow)

I ankled you to a grin, a

touchfeather glance.

I misunderstood.

    January.

        The sky hailed mothballs—

            I stand by the Vietnamese,
            arm in crucifixion.

I am no Petrarch, but in my dream, in your
words I love dogly pure,
sure that your
    rim of eye will
        turn.

I take my message
    wrapped in a cloud,
    dropped like a sink of helium on your
        doorstep.

A Chinese proverb says to
        know and not to
            act is not yet to
                know.

Love is

        imaginary improvisation,
            duet or solo.

(I beg mercy,
crave your gaze, a
        bowl of eyeballs,
                black, in my hands —

    the eye candy man.)

Parts of the passage in italics refer to the myth of the Ganges river, and its descent from the heavens.

Hampi (Ruins)

Columns in a temple
made of griffin, serpent, lizard,
gargoyle eye, elephant tusk, animals in
fold of gods,
firebreath fuming—
dancers, demons, devas,
flowers, crystals,
a sacrifice sowing the
celebration of priests who
lead a procession,
madly singing the earth to motion.

You stood in that universe
(hair in bun, nose in ring),

your hands stretching out to
catch a shower of sunlight
in an open palm,

on that winter afternoon.

In the evening, we sat on that hill
watching molecules
of green, brown, yellow, blue—
shades of the plumed snake—
settle to a setting sun,

palm trees, pagodas, boulders,
a clear sky —

we watched, and burnt
in the flames of a history that
bore the world, a
flicker
in our hearts,
our bodies trapped,
shaking like
      beasts in heat.

Garden, Bangalore

Two lizards —

wet from dew, a
cracked cosmos —

hop small over
       stone slabs

           (stabbed with shades —
                curtains of red —
                     these stones —
                         little Rothkos)

sitting still —

a monk brooding beside a
       solitary plum tree —

a large black ant
       watches solemnly

this little ripple, this
           wave of a hand, this
                click of an eyelash.

Still Life: Artichoke

Inside an art—
    i—choke:
        cave of mirrors,
            creased petals,
                vulva.

Triangle

You slit the two of us,
yin'yang.

Borrow our broken hands —
unleashed — to
cup your breasts.

You watch us with your fish eyes, your skin
veined in red.

Stab our backs with
cigarette burns on your tongue,

til we sink in stones 'fore you.

  *

On your magic carpet, in a
coliseum of artefacts —
spears, leopard skin, skulls —

we play games of chance,
dizzy with guilt.

(Hush... the Emperor my friend, white as
 elephant tusk,
  sleeps.)

*

Yesterday,
in the hope you'd
dance your dreams again,

I watched you
hurtle down the wooden stairs to
catch a falling feather outside your window.

I'm glad you still believe.

Shoreditch Serenade

She blinks —
I was burned outta the Royal Oak, closing time.
I glimpsed a crack in the glass, which grew to
        spider legs.
Winter buds waited for springsap,
        dressed like Chinese lanterns.

            Hanging from branches.

Last night, my friend, we made the end of a
story — as usual, you were late. I
held my cell like a
        crucifix to watch you
            stumble towards me in the
                coal of a London street.

            ~

He thinks —
I'm not sure. Never am.
        I drink to be animal.

At home in a piss-soaked alley off Kingsland Road, I
clock a rubbersmell pinot grigio, jiving to
        Bombay underground.

To build faith, I flagellate my
        bloodliver, a believer on Muharram.
               God will fasten my plea,
                       chainspike my flesh-hide.

I whistle, crippling to meet you on Columbia Road.

              ~

She hones —
I hurled you
        into my arms, the
                cat in my voice a queen.
You, ever in reserve, shied.

Around us, East London took effect —

      a Pole, two Sicilians, married, two Greeks drinking Cobra beers,
          fang in hand, Emily the Scouse violinist, a German who
                    thought Berlin too small.

As we floated like
        bottletops, scrap-paper, haymoss,
towards the estuary where Bethnal Green meets Brick Lane, I
        felt I'd lost my wallet.

                I, artisan.

              ~

He groans —
you order me, again, to
      glen them to a bar where two summers ago Naphtali
          spun me in axes.
                (You'll be there in a minute, you say.)

I lead your followers past bagel shops, hookah bars, offlicence
                              glory,
  cops prowling, the becoming dinosaur of the overhead rail, the
      bombed remains of
      cheap vinyl, soggy crêpes, torn jeans, pillpoppers.

      I am a helicopter.

      ~

She streaks —
cityboys them fucked off.
As I walked towards you, ma money in ma pocket, through
      graffitishocked streets, colours
          bled me with the damp of a morning star.

      Squatters them sclattered in the
          dungeon of a broken house, peeled windows.

      Some paint on scorpio bodies. Others hiss on cheap blow.
          My eyes trance in red 'n' green shapes.

      ~

He seeks —
hood of speed makes way in the bar —
    costume crunched, mascara masked, bass heavy
    ballsweat tinge of fahrenheit.
        Junkheads dance like coins tossed.

Russian at the crystal counter, studying film, winks through a
                                            funnel.
Athenian blathers on opera.
I shade my way to the plastic of the street, where I miss the Punjabi bouncer who
    spoke in cricket.

A musician, close from Chicago,
    beat-boxes me to movement 'n' sound. A
    Mama from Sao Paolo
        souls to rhythm. A
    dread-man looking like a lost friend, calls her posh,
        sings like it is, showing
        me his needles.

You emerge, glow from dew.
    Your breasts are temples.

        ~

She grooves —
gin and tonic fought me off, shook me solid. I
    spoke of Ghatak, hoped you'd understand. You
    dropped on your back, flailed like an

    alligator's tail. I
    balked, my lips forming soot.

Our friends grew ghosts on their backs. A
vomit of people gathered on the road. The
Spanish, who lock the afterhours scenes,
ritualed in fluorescence, deep in Commercial Street.

I motioned us — all of us —
    back to my den, a lion.

~

He hooves —
on your bed, I watch Emily play with Grotowski with
    crackedglass tooth. He no let her go, and she
    sinks in his shipsoil. They
    fall on tiles, solving politics.

    Sao Paolo's husband calls her a black cab back to Chancery
                                                     Lane.
    Chicagoman takes Hackney Wick by storm.

I tell you my life is a Lou Reed song.

I carve it out for you, a turkey.
                      I make an offering, in pollen.

~

She grins —
they went, you stayed,
    proud.

Sun slivered to the room, I watched the
    shyness bloom you.

I gave balloons, pinked you to health.
Washed you in stars.
Held you strong as cradle.
    Milked you to leave.
    I'll see you again, I oceaned, my
        teeth heavy with lead.

    ~

He sins —
overhead, sky forms a light-wedge.
Construction cranes in the distance
gleam like flamingoes. On Fashion Street, orange sun, sari-red
        clouds
    roll towards me in four horsemen. I hear
      thunder lift like elephants. A woman in veil
        slits towards me, her eyes cry as knives.
          She keels herself, kneel in chin, summoning
                God in trousers.

I am sane in tortured times.
      I dream your salt.
          You are gone.

IV

Nagri

(City)

Prologue/novel

for Jared Stanley

In an open field, chrome city streets. Blackhead pus of cars circulate round New Alipore golchakkar. Excavate gutters, fisheyed. Estuary of streets, five rivermeeting, holy water. Necklaceshaped streets, comfortably closed in by shops and stores of endless kinds selling groceries, electricity, fresh goatmeat, flowers, wine, cutlerycrockery, armchairs laced with silk dragons, telephone cards, marketed music, magazines, pets, paints, wallpaper, midget fashionwear, lampshade gas chambers, violin vultures, rubberplant fans, cowfart methane, crocodile plants, fresh humanmeat gingerspiced, leather eyes in boil, chandeliers, ice cream, glue, fresh hothot cars, jewels in ice, illegal immigrant-American alien-stamp you on forehead- barcode your balls-and-soul silicon chips, newspapers, health and safety global warming instructions, hotnsoursoup, kitfo, spicy chaat, cricket bats, milk massage, bloodpressure monitors, dialysis edges, psychiatrist, autoeroticality, laughing Bamiyan buddhas, frozen fishheads, neatly packaged Qurans, calligraphy flowerpots.

Maximum megalopolis, futurecity. Its walls plastered with communist propaganda, sickle 'n'chain, hammered light, nebulous neon, jeans, massshipped and shaped botox being, shirts and evening gowns stepping into dark bars, streets of cement littered with nondegradable plastic, starving stomachs running like dogs for shitstained bread, computer parlours teeming with paranoid atoms, subway stops sucking in omega supernovas, brick buildings

Kalagora | 73

with grilled and thatched windows, glass buildings vomiting suitedbooted workers, buses bleeding, cars hipping, rickshaws and trams, menwomen white-black-brown-blue, street musicians transnational incorporated, guitars, ektaras, djeridoos, pots, pans, electric wires, cockroach antennae, stretches of steel, cosmic cafe spots, cigarette colour cholera, balloon stomach dysentery.

Estuary of streets, five rivermeeting, holy water. New Alipore golchakkar. Dogman with dog around. Anarchists assemble, watching. Dog grows fangs, body skinned the colour of brown mud. Tail tattered, paper peeling. Ribs tensed like sharkmoves, bloody. Dogman master, loses control. Chain splits, voice curdles like milk. Dog revolts, anarchists clap. Dogman shuffles, calls out like a slavetrader, orders immunity. Dog dynamites. They both, ringed by onlookers, prey each other, circling. Dogman reaches, hands stretched to canine drips. Dog dynamites, bursts like a landmine, cannonfires, chop chop. Tears off the man's face, rips with cartilage bleeding. Man howls. Fights dog. Dog tears his face off, again. Man becomes Christ, momentarily. Bombs explode, horse appears.

Man chases dog on a horse. Megalopolis fuguehorns into cracks of light. My dream becomes a circle.

Animal City

I

Twin-bride of my ten-head home, I
    watch you closely from the
        cross of scorched lands, rubble of sea-foam,
            fire of snake-tongue.

Grand and pungent in act, I long to write you an epic
    worthy of our ancient tales.

For now, these
    bites will do, as I
    chrome myself round your lingo,
scalding my brow with your
    tears of grime, shame, bigtalk wealth.

I gender you in full-on
    curry angrezi, with
    patois political, image transcontinental.

II

Close on nine years you
    be my multiverse, *Bombay meri jaan*.

Now me your bastard
        ratshipper, who you coldthaw by turns,
        breaking limbs, tossing one by one after
                chop-'n'-changing me to your

dogs that bark the
        rounds of Kala Ghoda.

Me you fat in slums stomach-lining
        Chatrapati Shivaji International Airport,

me you snatch like the sea necklace by
        Marine Drive,

me you step underfoot towards the
        mosque that grows from the sea, by
        Hajiali, breakin me into the south.

Me you bleed on treetops that crown Siddhi-Vinayak,
        pole-vaulting through cricket parks, churchbells,
                                    lion in Sion.

Me you gorge in dark Bandra sounds,
        with India electronica, the asli bhangra.

Me you lick in clamour bars of Juhu,
        palm trees and pork by the sea-view.

Me you sweat in pav bhaji streets, pani-puri

gag, vada pao itch.

Me you wet in tobacco nights, incense from
    Nigerian peddlars in Colaba, fevered.

III

You are my crude health, the
    crass in my conscience.

(Once, one of your statue saints called out, at the
    curve of Mahim, as the smog of sun
    cut through canopy trees in
cockroach antennae: 'Life's an echo. You get back what you give.')

I remember too much. I insurrect. I thaw.

IV

Recalling me pulling out ear-wax,
    galling me, heavy and brown and long like rat shit, by
    Cuffe Parade at the ballpoint pen-tip of South Bombay.
    I see through large French windows, fishing-nets, seasalt.
        wood smells like horse-hide.

On the bus back to Versova, home from school, my
    Math teacher yells me bout

   them Goan sausages, how spicy they be, my
     mother would like them.

My first love, Aditi, in the school closeby
   Amitabh Bachchan's house. I thought her an
   androgyne, as in my child-wet dreams, we'd
     fly over electric grass, whitelight in Andheri.

But no no, I tell it straight, one
   image stark stays, genuine.

  V

We stop on Linking Road in days when Fiats
   clogged the shape of traffic towards Mahim Causeway.

Long before the whip of olive bars, mojo melts, too school for cool
         drawl-mocking
Mumbaikars, sultry and bangled Bandra girls.

No, back in the '80s, a few years before I
   played football with a bat-blind cancered grandfather, my
   mother 'n' me stop at the corner where Waterfield Road
       spills.

(Nearby, Maa liked the cottage-cheese shop.)

As we wait for the green light, a

sadhu six-footed walks to my openaired window,
dreads-matted, beard in forest, saffron-covered with
hint of charcoal, fume, lavender.

Him have a sleek, spotted,
jazz-patterned python wrapped round his
upper torso, fitted perfect like a bride's sari. The snakehead
juts out
in a slither above his locks.

He stretches them crow hands, pigeon nails,
towards me, eyes fired, jaundiced yellow.

I recoil, screaming. A
hijra on the street-divider claps his hands,
clacks like a witch. Light greens, cars cough, cop
blinks. Maa shakes.

VI

Them surrealists were hacks, term-tablers, scabs on a
tired, southern Europe.

They never knew you, O animal city, where a thousand gods
jostle like men hanging outta late-evening suburban trains,
rowdy, brutal, bleeding.

Now some call you Mayanagri, but in me—

    traitor—you be the slick oil, the
    steel breath, the becoming cancerous starshape of a
        fresh from sleep, proud,
                seething century.

'Mayanagri' translates, popularly, as 'city of dreams'. A 'hijra' is a eunuch.

Finding Time

In the evening
he — blind as Dhritarashtra — sits with eyes closed
midst shadowed rocks.

Hears the sun
ravish a brimming, boiling ocean.

Watches the sound of a sitar
make sparks fly off like flies
on a carcass of wood
by a house somewhere in the hills,
somewhere in the north —

a woman in white linen.

A young girl with jasmine eyes.

The scents of eucalyptus trees,
wet pigeons, candles.

The settle of a shroud.

Cold skin of a memory.

Chinatown, New York

A nose for paradox
made me read Chuang-Tsu
on a late autumn afternoon
in Washington Square—

from his butterfly dream
I too emerged with wings,
a flowing gown of red and green,
a taste for wet fingertips.

I wafted down Mott Street—
bees in my hair,
pollen on my tongue,
rain coiling in my eyes.

From your curious castle, heavy,
in a bowl hammered out of lapis lazuli,
you gave me thick soup
cooked in the entrails of a fatted fish —

strands of the Milky Way
welcoming, cradling me
from the sluggish approach of
snow, heating bills, a fading lover.

Benares

I'd wanted a horse-sacrifice.

Back then, they'd chop it to pieces on the steps of the Ganga. Slice the essential bits — eyes, hair, head, stomach, tail, leg, heart, skull, everything.

The horse

became a universe, a Mandelbrot set, fractalized. Horsehair was the fray of the galaxy. Circular spectrata in

queens cavorted with dead horses. Land's won. Anointed in wax.

Shiva, snaketongued father of mountain, came back in chariots of starlight.

I'd wanted to see this — the secret of cumcreation refle
xed in bubbles of fresh, boiling animal blood.

But no. For a week I get shit, instead. Mystical shit dripping every ooze o' the city. Dog shit, cow shit, goat shit, mosquito shit, monkey shit, guru shit, god shit.

I do the bits. Wake up to arti-sounds at five in the morning, watching the river heave in glorious filth. Voices, ethereal, sting like desert scorpions.

I row with a boatman who tells me that widows are the gravest sin. My throat becomes a crocodile. I smile at him, light a smoke, imagining my mother.

Every evening, diyas float on the water. The city is a star-seed. Beauty rubs on my belly. I cup my hands, lick its hair.

At nights, I hear Hindustani classical in a place called 'ganga-fuji'. I eat veggie. Watch bits of India playing Kenya at the world cup. Smoke spliffs with a monkey who tries stealing my food.

I sleep with a woman I love, dreaming of dreaming another who I lost.

In the morning, I am photographed, blackwhited, reading Rilke, sucking out the gloom.

The coffee shields me, as I hop past 'dirty European hippies' (so said an American bartender, tendering his change like tequila shots). This could be some sanitised heaven, I grimp, as I slip to the trainstation.

But no, the shit returns in a stark surrealismus:

    on the tracks, mossed with ratbones, a heaving breathing
              biting cow,
    tail humming like turbines,
swaying like the hips of those buxom village girls in
    '70s sooper-dooper hits,

stalks his territory. The tracks are his kingdom.
On platform, a bedlam beggar, Poor Tom for sure, laughs the cow,
his
best friend, throwing bits of yellow leaves sliced in
tear-shapes.
In response, the cow

whips its tail harder, hunches like a cowboy, letting loose
thuds of black hail, multifaeces, which fall in brown dust.
lizards gulp, flies grow, as a man on a vespa, helmethooded
crosses into focus, platformed into sunset.

In shit, is my salvation.
In dung grows the lotus, O blessed Benares...

Portrait, Little Lane, Calcutta

Cricket on a
small black and white radio
      in a chai shop —

I buy cheap cigarettes,
      five for ten, filters ribbed in red,
      shake hands of oil

        (the owner has a broken
        black hole of tooth,
        swallowing flies,
        atoms of fogfilled winter air)

noticing a minuscule merchant
      on the spat-on sidewalk,
      legs crossed in a lotus,
      selling among other things —

a painting of a Royal Bengal tiger.

      An etching of Krishna in wood.

            A postcard picture of the
                Sidney opera house.

Istanbul, November, '03

Elegy

Yeats' city
of desire and imaginings
fell to its knees
five hundred and fifty years ago—

women raped, babies cudgeled, ears
pinned to brick walls,
tongues left
oozing on altar, on chalice.

Now,
we see little things again—

bombed streets,
lips kissing
idols of broken bone,
husk of dead men in
cemeteries, in sea,
in sky.

I stand here—bent,
in front of a neighbor's telescreen
waiting for rough reawakenings—

travels by sea, Pietà,
alchemy —

and I try to turn away
from an image spooled
in a loom —

a woman
coughs ashblood, fingers
wirespunked,
crater of mouth —
reminiscent of steps in *Potempkin* —
gunning shreds of saliva.

Mother's Lament

The Pietà is renewed —

she sits on a road skulled with tanks,
while green hills round this burnt bulletholed town
gape at her breasts — ripe as Arabian mangoes.
They hover over the lips of a young, frostbitten man.

His head is a clock.
His right arm, a bow.
His beard, shy.

She wonders, running her fingers, draped in blood,
on a parching forehead.
She wheels through the sky,
leaking bones:

'Oh, the shiver o' my spine,
the salt o' my eyes,
the beam o' the sun,
the love o' my life —

drink of this pure, fresh milk
and remember to say your prayers.
I cooked you biriyani today
and your aunt has sent you sweets.
I washed your clothes so you'd look a butterfly.

I saw the girl outside the chai shop,
the one who charmed your father na!
Remember?
Your friends wait to
play their awful games,
and your letters are in order.

(The general gorges nails, cuts in mud.
Struts through city-gates,
lotus in eye.
He plucked my tooth, betel-stained, for a souvenir.)

Tomorrow you must wash your hair;
you must read your books.

Tomorrow, I'll put you to sleep, my chand ka tukra.
I'll tell you many silly stories.

Remember to share your secrets
and I will show you, the world is
truly beautiful.'

V

Epilepsis

Sketching (slight return)

'Saintliness means turning pain to good account.
It means forcing the devil to be God.'
—Jean Genet, *The Thief's Journal*

I

'I'll pluck the gods outta your belly!' she claims
syncopated, a guzzle of rotgut liquor, filterless in a
circus of smokerings.

She's danced with kings, fairies, pimps, artists, gangsters,
toothless beggars in shadows of red. Her body crusts in sin:

'I gave head first in a Goa church,
flaked in coconuts. God never forgave.'

II

He, severed by thirteen years, listens quiet,
fumbled like a held cigarette.
She tales him, winds him in the snakeskin of her
long voyage, herstory in blood—
a lover stabbed looking for junk in DC (by a
dealer he called 'batman'), she
pounding the lower east side hunting

the same fume of coal, the lick of bone. She
pulling out a half-formed, head-shrivelled
child from the tunnels of her womb somewhere in Calcutta. She an
illegal alien in the united status-quo of america, forging social
                                              security,
scratch cards, undertable jobs, fly bynight lovers. She an animal,
                                             wriggling,
spitting, fucking in the great dungeon of the world.

She a Fellini film.
Her laughter pukes new beginnings.

She sold blank cassette tapes in Milan, stole
black 'n' white film from corner shops, while a man
played sax from an open shutter. In Brixton, long before the
                                             daddyfund
hipsters, she drowned in Vietnamese soup, reggaeing her
way through ganja avenues. In Iraq, she
juggled her men, body smelling of the Amazon.

Now, she has grown scabs in her mouth, freckles
on her eye. Voyaged more than Ulysses.

He watches her smoke like a gun, her nails
yellowed, dipped in whiskey.
He speaks punctuated, full-stopping his
thoughts in neatly arranged boxes.

'You were never scared?'

'Fear grows from preserving,' she commands.
'I make change. I happen.'

   III

The first time they made love, a boxwhite room with
green tiles, she clothed him in a white t-shirt. In
sweating sun, his skin sowed a river. Her smells
chlored the sky. Mud made their food, their rain.

When he coiled away, they both
stared shocked at the white shirt, now covered leopardlike
in spots of fresh blood.
   Godstains.

They looked, searched for the cause,
found only scarred vinyl, old monk rum,
a flooded ashtray.

He sat alone, scared. She combed through
her farm of hair,
whisked him in the whirl of her
arms, saying with the
calm of a nun, quoting from a book:

you are all that is beyond
and disappearing.

Lightning Source UK Ltd.
Milton Keynes UK
UKHW011834270320
360990UK00001B/66